Reviews
A W

The Trial Run

Lawanda is a great person. Love her spirit and she is a very very kind-hearted and helpful and Godly woman; easy to talk to when going through hard times like I've been going through issues in my life. She is a God send. Thank you and God Bless you!!!! - Arlena

---

LaWanda Parks penned "A Woman In The Making: The Trial Run" based on her life with an inspirational twist! She is a very powerful Woman of God who has a heart for women and confidently keeps her hand on the pulse of the women she's been assigned to! If you're a woman in waiting or in the making, this is a must read for you! - Nicky

---

A woman of integrity, excellence, honesty, power, and vision. A woman who sees with intentions and go for it, a woman who has a heart for God and gives all of her to him. Who's dream is being manifested to no return. She's gifted in many ways and one who anyone wouldn't mind calling a friend. A woman of value! A woman that carries Strength.. Amen! - Patricia

--

LaWanda Parks is a Purpose Driven Woman. I have witnessed her overcome many adversities in her life and at each blow she still remained to RISE. Her story is one of pure determination to overcome everything that has tried to overcome her. She won't stop or be stopped. She will continue to Rise and Shine and be a Beacon that will lead others to the light of their Goals, Visions and Purpose and ensure that as she has Succeeded they will also Succeed. Shes a Phenomenal Woman!!! -Rosalyn

---

The Visionary and founder of Women In the Making is a powerful child of God, a strong woman of faith but most of all, she's a warrior of Christ.

She's a woman who does not quit! La Wanda has a heart that is as pure as gold! There is nothing more beautiful than a Woman of God who is brave, strong and emboldened because of who Christ is in her. -Nikki

A Woman in the Making:

The Trial Run

by La Wanda Parks

Dear Reader,

If you are reading this, you are contemplating if this will be a good book for you to read.

Let me tell you a little bit about the origination of this book. Although this book is a short read, it took me about 20 years to write. Why? I was distracted by so many issues and people. In addition, I wasn't ready to meet YOU where you are. You see, I had a lot more maturing to do. I would not have been an example for YOU! God has a way of maturing us through trial and error. I have been matured and developed through may fires. I completed this book in pain and at a very low place in my life. I invite you to walk my journey with me. I am a woman that is imperfect, trying to make the best out of imperfect situations.

The assignments in this book are not for me but for YOU! We, as women, must endure a lot thoughout our lives. We are built tough, yet we hold emotions as though most do not understand. We're often FIXERS. We must distinguish what was NECESSARY and what was UNNECESSARY. In the midst of this transformation, both of the necessary and unnecessary times must be a period of molding and making.

I often wondered if ANY BODY COULD SEE ME?

I see YOU! I want to meet you on your journey. Come walk with me. Lets figure out if YOU ARE A WOMAN IN THE MAKING ON A TRIAL RUN!

Prophetess La Wanda Parks

These are my memories, from my perspective, and I have tried to represent events as faithfully as possible.

Copyright © 2021 LaWanda Parks

All rights reserved. No part of this book may be reproduced or used in any manner without the prior written permission of the copyright owner, except for the use of brief quotations in a book review.
To request permission contact
LaWanda_Parks@yahoo.com

Paperback ISBN: 9798598059852

Edited and Layout by: Danielle Radden

Table of Contents:

1. Can Anybody See Me? 9

2. Was it Necessary? 17

3. The ONLY Woman Versus the OTHER Woman 22

4. Married and Living Single 27

5. I SEE YOU 33

6. The War Within 36

7. A Woman in the Making: The Trial Run ... 42

About the Author 46

Can Anybody See Me?

In my life, I have always been a fixer. I never felt fulfilled unless I had someone to fix. I'm not sure why I developed this trait; maybe because at some point I needed fixing myself. Maybe being a fixer was a distraction from really realizing the void I felt if I wasn't fixing something or somebody. This trait of mine would take me on a long and painful journey.

Fixers are individuals that need to be needed. Why we need to be needed could be because we experienced a severe rejection from a person who we trusted, or from someone who we expected to be there at some point to fix, love, and accept us. There is one thing that I have learned over the years: being a fixer is a seed that is planted at an early age. One just doesn't get up one morning and desire or look for someone to fix. No, this is a seed that is planted young.

Most fixers get so burdened down with fixing other people that we lose ourselves somewhere along the way. We also miss most of our lives because we are so busy fixing other lives. Personally, I gained other peoples' burdens, issues, pains, troubles, dislikes, likes, bad decisions, and consequences—the list goes on and on. I can never really remember being accepted throughout my young years. I was the kid that everyone kind of looked past and over. Ridiculed most of the time because my parents were strict, and I did not do much socializing or meeting up as they call it. I was kind of one of those invisible kids. You know the kind of kid that no one knows is there or even cares is there. I kind of blended into the walls. To be truthful, I did not want to be noticed or even talked to. I just wanted to wander throughout my days just wondering if existing was all it was cracked up to be. I just needed to be needed. Maybe I would be important if I could help those that just needed someone to talk to for a little advice. But who would want to get advice from me? No one really noticed me or even knew that I existed. I just needed just one person to SEE ME!

I am the oldest of four children. In our household, everything was routine. Dad made the rules and we kind of went along with them;

no questions asked. Being the oldest often put me in positions that I hated to be in at home. I was held to a high standard with all those responsibilities. My siblings looked up to me. I often wondered why, because in my world I was invisible to many and unimportant to others. But one thing I did know how to do was to fix all their issues and quiet all their fears. I would get them out of certain situations with Mom and Dad. I would tell them what to say when faced with a spanking. I would set the atmosphere to talk as a family. I made being in a very strict household more bearable. I knew how to fix things even though I was feeling empty and inadequate all at the same time.

I would often wonder if life was supposed to unfold this way. I would daydream about being someone else, someplace else. This would bring me comfort in addition to making me feel like I was a part of a world that accepted me. I was in charge in this other world and I was able to change anything about it that I wanted. I would lie in bed at night, and whisper a little prayer to God, asking him to please give me a life in which I was accepted, not just by my siblings but by my peers—those people that I shared my young life with almost daily.

"Why me," I would ask God, "Am I not good enough?"

A Woman in the Making: The Trial Run

I would hear him say, "You are more than good enough. I gave my son so that you can live beyond your circumstances."

I can't say that I knew exactly what that meant, but those words gave me such a peace that I couldn't explain. I was 12 years old at that time, and I didn't know this person that my pastor and my dad would talk about. But one day, I would come to know him for myself.

Nothing changed in my life until I reached the tender age of 16. I was still unnoticed and experiencing rejection at an all-time high. It seemed worse, because at that age, life is all about friends and acceptance. I would hear girls talking about their boyfriends and I would hear the boys taking about their girlfriends. I would just stand from afar and listen while wishing I could be a part of their world instead of mine. I had a crush on this one boy—one of those crushes when two people just look at each other and smile while walking down the hallway at school, and then sometimes at church on Sunday. I felt acceptance with him; I belonged with him. He would stand by me in the hallway, and he would even talk to me! I was beginning to feel as though I was worthy. We would often sneak away to talk on the phone. Finally, someone seemed to get a glimpse of who I was. I was ready to allow him to see me—all my rejection and insecurities. I was happy, I was normal, I was like the other girls—I had a boyfriend! Maybe, just maybe, I was normal and someone could see me. On June 12, 1982 my world came crumbling down. I was sitting watching TV when I heard my mother scream on the phone. She asked the caller what happened? I watched my mama intently trying to figure out what happened.

Mother hung up the phone and called my siblings and me into the kitchen to inform us that my boyfriend had just drowned. My world changed. This is when depression was introduced to me, and depression would prove to follow me for the rest of my life. I never got over his death. I isolated all the more. I was in a dark place, and I would not come out for many years to come. Now I was dealing with rejection, low self-esteem, and depression (anxiety would make its appearance in years to come). The seed of suicide was planted.

I was so buried in so many negative emotions by the time I reached the age of 16 that I did not know my identity. I was searching for some sense of belonging, but couldn't find it. I began to become a robot—I needed to wind up just to complete my everyday tasks. I was just wandering, not existing. CAN ANYBODY SEE ME?

There were days when one emotion would bounce off the other one, but the strongest emotion was suicide. Suicide is very tricky. Suicide will tell you that things are much quieter on the other side of life. Suicide will tell you that you are better off dead than alive. Suicide will tell you that no one cares anyway. Suicide will tell you that you are a failure. Suicide feeds off inadequacy. Suicide creates a mirage for those that often experience so much rejection. Once a person has been sucked into this world of suicide shenanigans, it's hard to lead them out. Its best to catch the seed of suicide early.

What most people don't understand about suicide is the seed is planted in areas that are not noticeable by the naked eye. The seed is buried so deep in negative emotions that it is hard to spot. As the seed is watered by other negative emotions and people, the suicide spirit becomes more apparent, but many times it is too late to uproot it. Don't be mistaken, suicide is very cunning and sneaky. Suicide will be there, but you will never know until it's too late. Suicide has to be exposed because it plants in the mind of the young, because they only see what peers and negative people they encounter have planted for them. They cannot see who they can become, whether accepted or not. They are UNIQUE and SPECIAL, just not to all people.

People don't just wake up and think suicide! Suicide becomes a learned thought. These thoughts are often planted by others. It is up to the individual to cypher through negative words and positive words. For example, a person that may think that he/she is worthless because of past behaviors, an inability to live up to others' standards, or their appearance. Although an individual may struggle with their own thoughts, other people build on those thoughts with their own actions or their own words that demean the individual. Many of these individuals think long and hard about the feelings that haunt them daily. They spend a lot of time alone trying to find a positive word or two as a bridge back into a world that will accept them. Many times, this world will let them down. The world will only build on the negative thoughts that he/she already struggles with. This deep cave/hole is the place that they will find their acceptance, a place they can rationalize a reason to keep going. They struggle with their thoughts, often wondering if there would be more peace in a place called death.

Who would notice, right? Who cares? I don't fit in anyway. I'm worthless, I'm fat, I'm ugly. Life is too much for me to bear.

They look for rationalization to cope, but find none.

Have you ever been here?

Come on in so we can talk. I understand. I've been there. I'm in that dark place with you. BUT we can't stay long. We have to find you a way out of this mirage that you have created for yourself.

You see, you only see the negative things about yourself. Let's talk about five things that make you unique. Just five. Is five too many? What about three?

You see, even though I don't know you, I can think of three things right off.

(1) You are unique

(2) You are a survivor

(3) You are DESTINED. Destined to LIVE.

You have to be delivered from yourself first, and then people.

Do a challenge for me: Take one day at a time and speak just one positive thing. For every negative, speak one positive.

YOUR life is YOUR life. It doesn't belong to anyone else. Stand UP and take control. Today is the beginning of the rest of your life. Death is not the answer—it is the final chapter of your life.

IT'S TIME TO LIVE! Remember, one day at a time! By the way, all the negative words you thought were a lie. All the negative words people have spoken to you are a lie! Let's get out of this cave. You first. Keep on reading and I will see you at the end of this book.

Can anybody see you? I CAN!

Was It Necessary?

Have you ever looked over your life and realized that you had so many failures? Where did they come from? Were these failures a result of a bad decision or maybe someone else's bad decision? Do you ever think that maybe if you could have handled things differently, you would not have found yourself with a very bad outcome? Do you look at that failed marriage, failed relationship, addiction, rape, molestation, or any other situation that you had no control over, then ask yourself, "Why me?"

There wwere so many times that I would ask God that very same question. "Why me?" I was a single mother, in and out of relationships. Five children with three different baby-daddies. Each relationship left me feeling rejected and unworthy of love. I left a part of me in every one of those relationships (even the ones I don't mention in this book). You see, a woman loses a part of herself in every relationship that she enters. How, you ask? By having to please each one of the men that she enters into a covenant with. If you put a man over yourself, then you lose a part of yourself.

If you are like I was, I was willing to trade me for him. I can't even remember when I lost my total self. I only existed to please and feel accepted by a man. I accepted so many things such as disloyalty, abuse (all kinds), deceit, lies, and mockery. I was often used and belittled just to name a few (just interject your issue in). One relationship after another; I experienced so much hurt and disappointment that I allowed this omen to leak into all areas of my life.

My life was a disaster by the age of 25 and slowly deteriorating. I was in and out of shelters due to domestic violence in one of my relationships—I gave birth to my baby son in a shelter. I would even be forced to leave my children with ladies in the shelter that I didn't even know. I had to work to ensure we had a roof over our heads— it was one of the requirements in the shelter. I wouldn't stay on a job for very long because I just lost the desire to succeed. Did I mention that I had to give my oldest child to my parents due to my teenage pregnancy?

I had no direction or desire to do better. I was going nowhere in a hurry. Sad thing to say? I was a product of my storms and issues. I was shunned by my community, some family members, friends' parents, teachers, and church members. You see, what society failed to realize was that I was not a woman mentally or emotionally ready to have a baby. I was only a woman physically able to birth a child. I was rejected by those I trusted, those that were supposed to nurture me and guide me. I believe this was the seed that was planted and watered throughout my entire life. This opened the door to other struggles in my life.

To try to escape, I slowly began to drink daily—nothing heavy, maybe wine, beer, or E and J Brandy (if I wanted the hard stuff). The drinking only lasted for a season. I really didn't like the feeling of being drunk, so I had to find another out. I tried marijuana, but that wasn't my thing either. I was too naive to hand out and roll the joints. I couldn't find a place of solitude, so I found comfort in men. Whether we admit it or not, we sell ourselves short every time we lay with the wrong men. We are no better than prostitutes—we just don't walk the streets or charge for our services. We hide behind closed doors and perform the same acts. Yeah, I did that too!

A Woman in the Making: The Trial Run

WAS IT ALL NECESSARY? That question is for each individual. For me, yes! It was necessary. If not for that failed marriage, failed relationships, sense of rejection, constant hurts, pains, and disappointments, I would not be the woman who is broken, yielded, humbled, and focused, with the ability to identify with who I really am. The woman that was always inside of me began to emerge. Standing strong in my identity, no longer with a need to be accepted by a man (or anyone else as a matter of fact), I can accept me. I have gifts that started emerging during that time of development, which became my, "Was It Necessary" season.

I do not know your struggles or what you have had to endure, but one thing I do know is that EVERYTHING you have encountered was necessary for the MAKING, BUILDING, DEVELOPING, and MATURING of your purpose and destiny.

Take about 10 minutes to reflect over the difficult events in your life. Where are you now? What have you learned from those incidents? Are you a better person? Are you a stronger person? What do you have to offer to anyone who is currently facing what you have overcome? YES, OVERCOME!

Get UP! You have knowledge and experiences that someone else needs as they OVERCOME. I don't care what it is, make your pains NECESSARY for your family, community, and even a NATION.

WAS IT NECESSARY?

YES!

Everything that you have encountered was necessary for THE WOMAN THAT IS IN THE MAKING!

Congratulations! You have torn down a wall that the devil thought you could not kick down. I hear the Spirit of God saying, "Even NOW, I'm working for your good." He is NOW dealing with your molester. He is NOW dealing with that abusive husband/cheating husband. He is NOW dealing with that abusive parent. He is NOW dealing with ALL those men that used and abused you. But most of all he is NOW dealing with your UNNECESSARY—God is making all of your ANGUISH NECESSARY! PIVOT, TURN, FOCUS, and take UN away from UNNECESSARY and walk in your season of NECESSARY. Reach deep down and SHOUT! I feel it deep in your belly. Take your life back! Come on, NECESSARY. Let's shake, rattle, and roll. Let's keep it moving.

The ONLY Woman Versus the OTHER Woman

This chapter will be kind of tricky. You see, some women are ok being the other woman, but the secure place in a relationship is to be the ONLY woman. Now, women are so used to being the OTHER woman that they settle for it with a good excuse to protect their womanhood. They make it seem as though they are ok with being second. That is what it is—SECOND and less respected. The other woman will always get the leftover time, conversations, gifts, emotions, etc. THE ONLY woman will always get the entire package. Some women spend years not realizing the difference. These women settle. Let's tear down some walls in this chapter. What are the advantages of being the OTHER woman? Why are you comfortable being the OTHER woman? Are you afraid of being rejected as the ONLY woman? Do you find it hard committing? If so, why? We must move from OTHER to ONLY. Let's shake, rattle, and roll. Let's go!

Understand that the word OTHER is an alternative word. OTHER is a universal word with no real meaning. OTHER is inserted in a sentence when no other word is known to complete a sentence. In a list, OTHER is the item that doesn't fit. OTHER is used to describe something that has no defined category. You, as the OTHER woman, are factual, but HIDDEN. Nine times out of ten, the ONLY woman doesn't know about you, but you know about the ONLY woman. At least that is what he has the ONLY woman believing. Now, don't be mistaken, you are factual for the simple reason that he is able to connect with you on his terms and times. Oh, I hear some of you saying, "Well, I tell him when I am free. I run the show." No Ma'am, no matter how you put it, HE runs the show. Why do I say this, you ask? My sister, he runs the show. He has already set the stage. You just read and obey the script.

Now, don't think that being the OTHER woman has age restrictions. OTHER is an equal opportunity employer. There are some OTHER women in their matured age of life. Let's just say we are well within menopause stage. The only difference in a relatively older woman and younger woman is the fact that the older woman should have already defined OTHER vs ONLY!

To be fair about it, we might have recognized the game before he got a word out, but just allowed him to speak just to see where he was at. Conversation might not have been all that good, yet we allowed him to reside in our den too long. Most men do not capture a woman right off. We allow him to get in our space. Once you become the OTHER woman, you hold that position for a while after you get caught up. Regardless of what you do and say, OTHER woman, you are FACTUAL, but HIDDEN.

Allow your instincts to navigate you through your life of dating. I have often heard women say, as the OTHER woman, "Oh, he will never leave me alone!" Well, why should he if you are willing to stay as the OTHER woman. But are you comfortable that he can keep coming back with the pretense you don't require more than he is giving you?

He's probably getting out of your bed in the wee hours of the morning to go home or somewhere. Are you good with that? Let me deal with that issue. It is totally disrespectful for a man to come and use your body UP, yet leave before the sun comes up. Your body is worth more than that. I call that "the before the sun comes up" call! If you are going to do that, at least challenge him to breakfast. Will he stay? Don't get me mistaken, most of us need three meals to survive and sometimes a snack in between.

I'm just saying, if a man can shop for Macy's merchandise at the Dollar Store, trust and believe me, he will. Let him know, "This is not the Dollar Store—that would be down the street. You are now entering Macy's, and I am not having a half-price sale. Everything is marked at its original price." Don't let any man try to get you for less than what you are worth.

Why are you settling? I'm speaking to your inner person, "You are worth so much more." It doesn't matter what you look like, it doesn't matter what you have been through, it doesn't matter your education level, it doesn't matter your color, it doesn't matter your speech, and it doesn't matter your community stance. IT DOESN'T MATTER because at the end of the day, you possess EVERYTHING the ONLY woman does, except the title. If his ONLY woman can't satisfy his manhood in every aspect of it, he in the wrong place at the wrong time. You are not a SUPPLEMENT. YOU are the real thing.

I speak even now that your position is changing. I pray that God is removing the cover from your eyes. Stand UP, brush yourself off. You will no longer be accepted as the OTHER woman. Cross over the threshold from OTHER to ONLY! ONLY states that I know who I am, I am Confident in who I am, and I know what I bring to the table. If he leaves today or tomorrow, you will still be somebody's ONLY woman.

God loves you and wants the best for you. Whether ONLY or OTHER, you are special to God; with a purpose. I hear the Spirit of the Lord saying, "I'm doing a new thing in your life." He is giving you a new definition of your self-worth. I hear, "CHANGE, CHANGE, get ready for the CHANGE." There is a shift that will take place. PIVOT and FOCUS! This is your season. You are FACTUAL, but not hidden.

Let's shake, rattle, and roll. You are like NO OTHER. Say, "I am like NO OTHER!!!"

I feel some women coming out. Let your next conversation to that man be "I SEE YOU!" Change the scenery up. You know how! Most of the time, you let him make it anyway. I'm not sure he will be ready for the woman God has set free. Be gentle, kind, and humble, but move around. Unless he is exhibiting ONLY, he's wasting your time. There is a man that wants you as his ONE and ONLY! OTHER is not for you anyway. Come on, sister, let's move to the next chapter. You are going to be just fine.

Married and Living Single

Most girls reach a certain age when they daydream about marrying their prince or a knight in shining armor. They believe that their prince or their knight will sweep them off of their feet, and they will live happily ever after. Most experience that warm feeling inside as they wait for this special man to enter their lives. Of course, there may be a few disappointments while they wait.

Dating is an experience all within itself. We may find what I call a mix-match man. This means he possesses one or two of the traits we require, but he doesn't meet most of our requirements. We convince ourselves that no man is perfect, so we SETTLE. We come to find out that our requirements were compromised so we move on to the next man. However, when we move on, it always seems that we settled, lowered our standards, and wasted our time. We move on to the next prospect, and he seems to be just the right match. However, we find he is also a mix-match prospect. Again, we settled, wasted our time, lowered our standards, and lost valuable time.

This mix-match dating can take a toll on a woman. Many times, we begin to question ourselves and sometimes our self-worth. Maybe we even think that we will never find that prince or knight. We usually travel through a period I call "wandering." We wander from emotion to emotion. We wander from friend to friend for advice. We wander from self-help book to self-help book. We wander from man to man. We just wander—not out of curiosity, but out of self-affirmation.

Is something just wrong with me? Are my standards too high?

At this point of a woman's life, she becomes very vulnerable. However, during this season of her vulnerability comes that prince! He is so perfect, he passes all the tests. He is not a mix-match man. He says all the right things. The woman and her prince want the same things in life. He is different than all the rest. He opens the door for her, he holds her hand, he calls her all throughout the day, he sends her flowers, and he makes her feel like she is the only woman in the world. This is the one! This is the man that she is destined to marry. Her dream comes true and he asks her to marry him. The wedding she has always dreamed of becomes the wedding that everyone is talking about. The honeymoon is beyond her wildest dreams. Both of them have managed to be financially stable. The two of them may struggle, but their love and determination is her pillow.

It sounds perfect, but even a great marriage can suffer. Even if you have your prince, no marriage is easy. You may both be financially sound with great careers. However, what matters is your role within the marriage. A perfect marriage might change until it becomes two people living in the same household—married, yet living single. Let's talk about that.

Marriage is a bond in which two people share their thoughts, time, and emotions. Remember date nights, candle light dinners, and lying in bed talking and laughing? Remember being excited about him coming home from work, him bringing flowers, or his simple smile to show how excited he is to see you? You two were in your own world. Life couldn't be any better than this, but then you began living single. All of a sudden, he isn't excited when he comes home. He doesn't greet you with a kiss. He doesn't hold you like he used to. Intimacy is scarce. No more bed talks. No more date nights. No more planning the rest of your lives together. You push and try to rekindle things, but he seems to be too busy or preoccupied.

At first the change was bearable—year after year after year—until, one day, you find yourself empty and disappointed. What do you do? Now you have been married a few years, and you don't want to just walk away and have another failure. After all, he was your prince. So, what do you do? You go with the flow—living single, yet within a marriage. You start dating yourself; taking yourself to lunch, taking yourself to dinner, finding a new hobby, or a friend group. You start planning life alone, yet within this marriage. You go to bed alone; whether he is there beside you or not, you feel alone. You walk around the house with very little spoken. Now instead of talking to him, you talk with your friends or family members. Although there is a couple in the household, you both are living single within the title of a marriage.

What can I do? I'm married but living single.

I feel your disappointment!

What now? Do I just remain miserable? Do I stay in the marriage, living single? What will people think? What will people say? What will my church family say? He makes all the money. How will I live? What will my friends think? Can this marriage survive our time of living single?

I'm not sure of the answers to these questions. This subject is very tricky. No one should just step in and advise you to leave a marriage—that is out of order. Most people would tell you that they would have left a long time ago, or they will tell you what they would put up with. Girl! First step is to evaluate your partner's life and the marriage. If he is still in the marriage, rest and believe he has some issues, but you just don't know about them. Is there something in your marriage to fight for still?

My question to you is, "Are you happily married, living single?"

Take your time to answer that question. You have to really assess the question before answering. In the meantime, get to know yourself better. What makes you happy? What are your dreams and goals? But the most important question is, "Can you stand the rain?" If you feel as though your marriage has some substance and worth fighting for, put on your rain jacket, hold your umbrella up, and check the forecast to see how long the weather will last. It may be hard to weather this rain storm, so just ensure your rain jacket is leak-proof and your umbrella has no leaks.

Women have an inner instinct about how to fix something if it's FIXABLE. You don't need a manual! Dig deep. What is your instinct telling you? MOVE on it, but remember never move on

A Woman in the Making: The Trial Run

your emotions; MOVE according to your HEART and INSTINCTS. You don't have to be MARRIED, living SINGLE. It's your choice how you want to erase the single part. Married and single are opposite of each other, right. You can have one and not the other. You choose!

Get a pad and get to writing. What does God say about marriage? Let that be your foundation to begin your journaling. See you in the next chapter. Let's shake, rattle, and roll. Let's keep climbing!

I SEE YOU

This chapter should be fun. Let's talk a little about those people you thought were for you, but plotted your demise. You know what's funny about that? Most people that were against you were right next to you. You kept watching the people that you set at bay, because you knew they meant you no good, yet you missed what was right next to you. Mama used to say, "Keep your enemies close." Well, I was doing that, and didn't realize it.

You know, y'all, most of the time people don't like you because they are jealous of you. That darn jealousy is a powerful emotion and CANNOT be hidden. Jealousy will show its head sooner or later. How can another woman be jealous of another woman? Let's evaluate that. Maybe because she keeps her hair nice, her make-up's

A Woman in the Making: The Trial Run

always on point, she has a good husband, great job, and nice house, and ministry on the rise, just to name a few reasons. Some women just don't know why they're jealous of another woman. Let's look at that. We are not in the dressing room with their success. In other words, we do not know what that woman had to go through to get to where she is at. To be honest, most women don't care what the next woman had to go through to get that poised look.

Why are women jealous because another woman walks with confidence? Some would say, "She thinks she is all that." And maybe some women do think that—they are all that—but most walk with confidence because they know who they are, what they had to go through to get where they are, and they deserve where they are. No one can come for THEM to get it. You don't know it, but you have these same jealous-minded women—hidden, blending into the environment, meaning you no good. But I see YOU!

Look, let me go ahead and get to the meat of this chapter. Sometimes these women are on the inside to replicate you. Yeah, they want to clone you. They want to clone everything about you. They are secret intelligence enemies—they want the plans, but are not ready for the BLUEPRINTS. They want to know your next move. In all honesty, they are not ready for your world, because they did not pay your price. There cannot be promotions in life without paying the price. Are they really ready? They can never replicate a price that has already been paid—that's second-hand shopping.

Sometimes it's good to keep your enemies close, IF they will be an asset later. If not, put them with the outside enemies. Demote them, girl! Sometimes, we get tired of playing that game of I don't see you, yet you keep coming for me. The more you soar, the more the inside enemies come for you, but soaring is the best revenge. Just remain quiet, yet keep assessing whether you can benefit from them. They are taking up space for those that genuinely want to see you PIVOT, ASSESS, and MOVE!

Sometimes you even have to chuckle that they really believe you don't see them. Create a circle in which you don't have to watch who's right next to you. The next time you see that inside enemy that you KNOW is trying to blend in, wink at them, smile, and say, "I'm just beginning to SOAR, BUT I SEE YOU! Time for a DEMOTION."

The War Within

We, as women, struggle with so many areas in our lives. We must fight psychologically, emotionally, physically, but most of all mentally. Many times, we find ourselves in bad situations with our family, marriage, relationships, coworkers, and friends. Do you find yourself in the same situation with the same people, feeling the same emotions? Was it something they said? Was it something they have done? Was the outcome different than usual? Who was at fault? I was always told, it is not about WHO is right, but WHAT is right. Let's look at some things first.

Most of the time, when you are the common denominator concerning issues and situations, you are the problem. Let's evaluate the struggle. Many times, a person that faces issues as the common denominator, has issues that are going on within them. I call this the inward struggle. I will use myself as the example in this chapter.

I am a very guarded person. That's the nice way of putting it. I AM ALWAYS IN DEFENSE MODE. Can anybody relate? I am the type of person that analyzes everything a person says to me. I dissect every word. I always enter into a conversation waiting for the negative. I trust no one. I would enter my conversations with what I call a "Torn-Up Face;" my body language and face would link up in sync. My expressions would say, "Please don't come for me." I was ready for whichever way a conversation was going to go, but all my conversations went the same way—negative. I was an equal opportunity employer. No one was exempt. This kept me angry and bitter all the time. I would find the fault in everyone else, but could not see the erupting volcano in myself. Other people had the problems; I didn't.

Do any of these excuses seem familiar? *They came to me the wrong way. They said the wrong thing. They knew not to come for me like that. They were just wasting my time. I was just protecting myself. They knew better than that. They have issues.* The list goes on and on.

We do not realize we are the common denominator, because the situation and people change; we don't change. Why was I like this? I was a very angry person. Why was I angry? Everything and every person that had wronged me. I carried all that anger around in me. I never just sat and delt with me. There was a war going

A Woman in the Making: The Trial Run

on inside of me. It was easier to deal with the other person's issues rather than my own. To tell you the truth, I protected my issues because I felt safe in my anger. Crazy, I know! But I had created this world where anger was my solitude. Listen, when I say angry, I mean that I said what I wanted, when I wanted. There were occasions when I would self-talk before I would speak, but that didn't go over well. It came out sideways. All I would say was "OOPS, I tried." I would say very mean and hurtful things to people. My behavior ran really important people away.

I was sitting on my couch one morning listen to my worship music. I was meditating on this chapter of my book. God spoke these words to me, "Allow me to take away the heart of stone, and give you a heart of flesh!" I broke down and cried. He told me that many had stolen my ability to feel compassion. He told me that I was fighting against the plan he had for my life. I was behind time, because of the WAR that was going on within me. I could not let go of those that hurt me. I could not let go of those that deceived me. I could not let go of those that disappointed me. I could not let go of those that rejected me. I COULDN'T LET GO!

Lord, how do I let go. I pray and pray and pray and pray. I have the right intentions, but I always fail to yield to them. I am angry, I am hurt, I am disappointed, I am scared, I am confused, and I am broken. I want to be able to communicate with people with love, compassion, and understanding. I don't want to walk around defensive. I don't want to walk around miserable on the inside. I don't want to feel the war going on the inside of me. I don't want to protect myself with anger. I am tired of fighting ME. I am my worst enemy. The change begins with me! I must take a long look at ME. I must take my eyes off of everyone else and their flaws, and calm my own war.

I am not sure what war you are battling inside. You don't have to give in to everyone else around you, you just have to give in to your WAR. Put your flag up and say, "I surrender. My fight is not with any of you. My fight is with me."

What do I do now? I have identified my opponent. It is me. Where do I start? It's like I am standing in a lot of rubble, and I don't know where to begin picking up the pieces to clean up the mess. I'm tired of ME! I need to address ME! I am a mess! This WAR has landed a grenade inside of me, and I have exploded. I am torn up on the inside. I am smiling and communicating with people, but a grenade has just exploded inside of me. I'm torn up on the inside, but dressed down from head to toe on the outside. I got me a nice home, nice car, financial security, career on the rise, and ministry on the move. You might think I've got it all together. Only if you could take an

MRI of my insides, you'll see. I am at WAR with ME, and I am losing (some of you will get that a little later).

Let's bring this war to a truce here. I had to decide what I wanted to do with me. You have to decide what you want to do with you. How is this war on the inside affecting you and everyone that you come into contact with? Most importantly, are you the common denominator? You must answer these questions honestly. God will always expose YOU to YOU first. You may ignore it. That is when someone else will have the heart to expose YOU to YOU. I had both enlightenments—God and a special someone who exposed me.

If you are at the stage of wanting to settle the war, then it's time to begin your recovery program. Look around you. What does your battle ground look like? Are there a lot of dead bodies (people that you have hurt due to your war)? What about the fallen soldiers (The people that tried to help you, but you hurt them with your rejection)? What about your ranking authorities (God, your pastors, your women's groups)? Who won the war? Suite up, and let's do the work. First of all, you must begin by letting things go. Let the people that hurt you go! How much time have you lost? Your battle ground shows defeat! You were defeated a long time ago. You just had to recognize that you were at war with yourself.

Surrender YOU so that you can live. Pick up that second grenade that was about to blow, and throw it as far as you can! *Not this time, devil. I am aware of the war. I am about to surrender myself and everything that includes me.*

You are so much more beautiful and pleasant after the war. Straighten your crown! It looks good with your camouflage. Let's move, warrior. We have some work to do! You are now one with the War Within.

A Woman In the Making: The Trial Run

Well ladies, I am about to bring this book to a close. I have given you what God has given me. I already had the life experiences; He just had to put it all in order for me to give to you. I have been through so much in my life. I could not understand the concepts at first. To be brutally honest with you, I wasn't mature enough to talk to each of you. I was in the process of development and maturity myself. See, so often we want to rush purpose. Purpose comes with a price, and yet brings so much success. We just have to abide by PURPOSE's rules.

Everything that I have gone through had its rightful place. I still have the battle scars, as most of you do too who are reading this book. If it had not been for the beatings, the rejection, the betrayals, the wars inside, the disappointments, the sleepless nights, the failed marriages, the failed relationships, the homelessness, the suicidal thoughts, the teenage pregnancy, the single motherhood struggles, and most of all the nomad wandering, I wouldn't be as strong and focused as I am today. I just had to go back and put the pieces of the puzzle together. See, putting a puzzle together takes strategy. You can't force a piece of a puzzle where it doesn't go. Your pieces must fit perfectly. Every trial has its perfect place.

For that single motherhood piece of the puzzle, I am now the CEO and Founder of "Women In The Making Ministries." For that rejection and emotional trauma, I have begun a forum for those suffering from anxiety called "Brook Cherith." As a testament for other women, I have founded "Redeemed Christian Life Coaching." For all those psychological traumatic events, I have achieved 71 accredited hours in psychology. Because my children and I went without and were considered poverty-stricken, I am in the process of achieving my realtor's license. Because all of my struggles were NECESSARY, I now can publish this book.

Don't get it twisted—this is just a TRIAL RUN. I will be back with a workbook for you! I paid the price for you already, so you could read this book. There is no balance-owed. It is time for you to step forward toward your dreams and goals. You have gone through too much not to PRODUCE through your pain. PAIN should always produce DRIVE.

This book is not for me; it is for those coming after me. I am called to whoever reads this book. Find out who and what you are called to. I want you to begin to testify to other women about your victory. Our saying will be, "YOU ARE SIMPLY A WOMAN IN THE MAKING ON A TRIAL RUN!" Walk up to a woman that seems to be in her process, and tell her "Get Up, Girl. YOU ARE SIMPLY A WOMAN IN THE MAKING ON A TRIAL RUN!"

To all of you, your PURPOSE has just collided with your DESTINY, and it is working in your favor. I challenge you to get all the contamination out of you today—tonight. Tomorrow is a new day. After reading this book, I decree that life as you know it will never be the same. Breathe, because I will be back. This book was simply about A woman in the making on a TRIAL RUN!

La Wanda Parks

About the Author

La Wanda Parks was born and raised in a small town called Bay City, Texas. La Wanda has 3 other siblings of which she is the oldest. She got saved at the tender age of 13. Her journey of living saved would prove to be the foundation of her ability to climb. La Wanda had her first baby girl at the age of 16, and her second baby girl at the age of 18. Her family grew even larger at the age of 21 when her first son was born. Another son was born to her at the age of 24. The last son would be born at the age of 26. La Wanda raised her children as a single mother. There were multiple relationships and two marriages between the birth of her five children. All those relationships failed including the marriages. The one relationship that did not fail was her relationship with God!

La Wanda was able to overcome Domestic Violence, Emotional Abuse, Homelessness, Depression, Anxiety, Rejection, and thoughts of suicide as she balanced single motherhood. There were often times of loneliness as she battled these issues. La Wanda has developed a drive that allows her to kick in doors that were closed to her due to her circumstances. Her accomplishments vary from being CEO of Women In The Making Inc, which is a Non-Profit Organization founded for Young Single Mothers and Empowering Women, 71 Accredited Hours in Psychology, and CEO of Brook Cherith which is a forum created for those facing Anxiety. La Wanda is a certified Christian Life Coach. She continues to work on her Real Estate License, and currently works as Executive Director for a Housing Authority.

You can reach La Wanda by email at

LaWanda_Parks@yahoo.com

Acknowledgements

La Wanda states that her relationship with God and her five children kept her focused, with the ability and strength to write this book. La Wanda also has a special mention for a special man that motivated her to keep striving. Lord, I thank You for seeing me worthy to write this book for the person that is now reading it. Tinequa, Shinequa, Dezmon, Ben Jr, and Demion, INCLUDING ALL 21 OF MY GRANDCHILDREN! Thank You All for being my driving force. Most of all Thank You, Reader for allowing me to be a part of your journey! We are simply A Woman In The Making On A Trial Run!

.

Made in the USA
Columbia, SC
15 March 2021